Budget
Like a Boss:

STRAIGHT-TALK GUIDE TO MASTERING YOUR MONEY

STRAIGHTFORWARD MONEY ADVICE FOR EVERY CHAPTER OF YOUR LIFE

Aaron B. Kershaw

Copyright

Budget Like a Boss:

Straight-Talk Guide to Mastering Your Money

© 2024 BuildingBlocs Publishing & Aaron B. Kershaw

All rights reserved.

2nd Edition: 2026
ISBN: ISBN: 979-8-90345-001-5

Aaron B. Kershaw

BuildingBlocs Publishing
Raleigh, NC

aaron@buildingblocs.org

Disclaimer:

This guide is intended for educational and informational purposes only. It is not a substitute for professional financial advice. The author is a licensed financial advisor; however, individual financial situations vary, and the content in this guide should not be construed as personalized advice. Always consult with a licensed financial professional, such as a CPA or financial advisor, before making any significant financial decisions. The author and publisher are not liable for any actions taken based on the information provided in this book.

Printed in the United States of America

Table of Contents

Introduction

Hey there, future money masters! My name is Aaron B. Kershaw, but you can call me Uncle Aaron; most folks do, especially when they need advice that doesn't come with a side of judgment. I've had a colorful ride through life, complete with enough twists and turns to make a roller coaster jealous.

I've run different types of businesses; produced a radio talk show (yes, my voice can charm the pants off a dial), and spent over 25 years capturing life's moments as a professional photographer and videographer.

As a father of four, I've learned that managing finances feels a lot like herding cats; just when you think you've got it all together, someone decides to go rogue and blow their allowance on the latest video game or trendy sneakers. I've been married and divorced, and I'll tell you, nothing teaches you about financial responsibility quite like splitting assets with someone who thinks avocado toast is a breakfast food worth spending on every day.

But here's the deal: no matter how many life lessons you rack up, there's always room for growth. In 2018, life tossed me back into the classroom, and let me tell you, being the oldest guy in class is a blast; especially when your classmates are fresh-faced and haven't yet discovered the joys of student debt. I realized quickly that even though I had some savvy under my belt, I still had a lot to learn about managing money without losing my mind.

I went on to earn a **Bachelor of Science in Business Management**, with a focus on *Finance* and *Economics*, through the **VA Veterans Vocational Rehabilitation Program**. I'm also a **licensed financial advisor** and former operations partner who assisted in managing over $600 million in assets at Ameriprise Financial Services.

I hold **licenses in various types of insurance**, including *life*, *health*, *property*, and *casualty*. This isn't just theory for me; I've been in the trenches and seen how proper financial management can change lives.

This guide is my way of helping you avoid the pitfalls I stumbled into; like that time I bought a fancy coffee maker, thinking it would save me money, only to realize I was now just brewing overpriced coffee at home. I'm here to walk you through budgeting in a way that doesn't feel like a punishment or a math test.

Budgeting isn't just about avoiding debt or saving pennies;

it's about gaining the control and flexibility to live your life without constantly worrying about your bank balance.

So, grab a seat, and let's dive into the world of budgeting with some laughs and practical tips. Together, we'll make sure you're not just surviving but thriving; without the anxiety of being one unexpected expense away from disaster. Let's get started!

Introduction to the Series:
BUDGETING AND BEYOND

Introduction: This Isn't Just a Book - It's a System

Let's get one thing clear right from the start.

This is not just another financial book.
And you're not stepping into a collection of disconnected materials.

What you are holding is part of a complete learning system developed under *The BuildingBlocs Group* - designed to help you understand money, apply it in real life, and build a financial approach that actually works.

Because the truth is simple:
Most people don't struggle with money because they lack discipline.
They struggle because they were never given a system that makes sense in the real world.

This was built to change that.

The BuildingBlocs System
The BuildingBlocs system is structured to move you beyond information and into real-life application. It is supported by four divisions, each playing a specific role:

BuildingBlocs Publishing
Where the knowledge begins. This division produces over 100 titles focused on financial literacy, life skills, and real-world education.

BuildingBlocs Academy
Where learning becomes structured. This division trans-forms book content into guided, hybrid learning experiences designed for practical use.

BuildingBlocs Literacy
Where research, curriculum development, and editorial stan-dards are created. This ensures that all content is aligned, structured, and built for long-term impact.

The BRIGHTPath Foundation
Where the mission is carried forward. This foundation expands

access to underserved communities, veterans, and organizations seeking financial education and life skills training.

Together, these divisions form a single purpose:

To help individuals move from understanding information... to applying it in real life.

HOW THE SYSTEM WORKS

This system follows a clear and practical progression:

Learn it.
Apply it.
Make it your own.

Step 1: Learn the System

Money Adventure: Your Guide to Financial Freedom

This book provides the foundation.

It introduces how money works; from financial habits and mindset to budgeting, saving, debt, income, and long-term planning. It is designed to give you a complete understanding of the financial landscape so you can make informed decisions moving forward.

Step 2: Apply It with Guidance

Budget Like a Boss – Hybrid Course (BuildingBlocs Academy)

The course brings structure to what you've learned.

Built from the core principles of the financial system, it walks you through the process step by step, helping you stay consistent, accountable, and focused. It is designed for those who benefit from guided learning and practical application.

Step 3: Personalize It to Your Life

Budget Like a Boss (Book and Companion Workbook)

This is where the work becomes personal.

These materials help you apply the concepts directly to your own situation; your income, your expenses, your goals, and your stage of life. They are designed to turn knowledge into a working system that fits your reality.

Because financial planning is not one-size-fits-all.
Your life stage, responsibilities, and goals all matter.

WHY THIS APPROACH WORKS

Most financial resources stop at information.

This system does not.

It is built to move you through three essential stages:

Understanding – learning how money works
Application – putting those principles into action
Ownership – building a system that works for your life

This is where lasting change happens.

Final Thought

You do not need to have everything figured out to begin.

You do not need to be perfect with money.

You simply need a system that makes sense; and the willingness to take the next step.

This was built to give you both.

COMING IN 2026...

MASTERING MONEY:
(BOOK 4)

Overview: This second book takes you deeper into financial management. It's all about overcoming debt, building wealth, and planning for major life goals. Through actionable advice and strategies, you'll learn how to make your money work for you.

Key Takeaways:

- Smart debt management using snowball and avalanche methods.

- The magic of compound interest and how to start investing.

- Strategies for big life goals like homeownership, education, and long-term financial security.

Who It's For: Readers ready to take their financial understanding beyond the basics and start building wealth.

A PERSONAL INVITATION

This series is more than a guide; it's a partnership. I've walked this path, and I'm here to walk it with you. From basic budgeting to financial independence, each book is designed to meet you where you are and take you where you want to go.

So, grab a cup of coffee (or your drink of choice), settle in, and let's start this journey. You've got this; and I've got your back.

Chapter 1

Budgeting for Singles

YOU'RE FLYING SOLO

Being single has its financial perks; you have full control over your money and don't have to worry about anyone else's spending habits. But the flip side is that you're responsible for all of your expenses on your own. No one's splitting the rent, contributing to the bills, or sharing the costs of groceries. This chapter is all about how to manage your money when you're flying solo, and how to set yourself up for financial success as a single person.

DEVELOPING FINANCIAL DISCIPLINE

OVERCOMING EMOTIONAL SPENDING

Managing your money effectively as a single person also means understanding your emotional triggers around spending. It's easy to fall into the trap of retail therapy, spending money impulsively to make yourself feel better after a rough day or splurging because no one is around to hold you accountable.

Recognizing Emotional Spending

What is emotional spending? It's when you buy things based on your feelings rather than your needs. This might happen after a stressful day at work or as a way to celebrate a small win. Emotional spending can quickly throw your budget off track, especially when it becomes a habit.

Tip: *"I used to splurge on things like new gadgets or nights out with friends just to feel good after a long week. But in the end, I realized that those purchases weren't worth the financial stress they caused later."*

Overcoming Emotional Spending

- **Identify Triggers**: Keep a journal of your purchases and how you felt before making them. Over time, you'll notice patterns that trigger emotional spending.

- **Create a Waiting Period**: Before making any purchase over a certain amount, give yourself 24-48 hours to think about whether it's necessary.

- **Set Financial Goals**: Having clear goals, like building an emergency fund or saving for a vacation, will help you resist emotional spending and keep you focused on what's truly important.

ANECDOTE:

LEARNING THE HARD WAY

"Back in the early 90's, when I was running my towing business, I thought I was invincible. Money was rolling in, and I was spending it just as fast as I was making it. New equipment, nights out with friends; it all seemed like no big deal at the time.

Then, one day, my truck broke down. Suddenly, I had a massive repair bill staring me in the face, and I didn't have an emergency fund to cover it. I had to scrape together what I could, take on extra work, and borrow from friends.

It was a huge wake-up call that if I didn't start budgeting and saving, I'd be in big trouble when the next crisis hit. That was my first real lesson in financial discipline, and it changed how I approached money from then on."

Action Plan for Singles

When you're on your own financially, it's essential to build good habits early.

Here's how to start:

1. Follow the 50/30/20 Rule

One of the easiest budgeting methods for singles is the **50/30/20 rule**:

- **50% of your income** goes toward needs like rent, groceries, utilities, and transportation.

- **30% of your income** can be spent on wants, like dining out, entertainment, and travel. Yes, you're allowed to enjoy your money!

- **20% of your income** should go toward savings, including your emergency fund, retirement, and investments.

This rule helps you cover your basic needs, while also allowing for some fun and ensuring you're saving for the future.

2. Automate Your Savings

Saving money doesn't have to be hard. Set up automatic transfers from your checking account to your savings account so that you're saving money without even thinking about it. Consider splitting your savings into different accounts:

- **Emergency Fund**: Aim for 3-6 months of living expenses.

- **Retirement Savings**: If you have a 401(k) through work, make sure you're contributing at least enough to get any employer match. If you don't have a 401(k), consider opening an IRA.

By automating these transfers, you're ensuring your future is secure without having to actively make the decision each month.

3. Start Building Your Emergency Fund

Life has a way of throwing curveballs, and an emergency fund is your financial safety net when something unexpected happens; whether it's a medical bill, car repair, or job loss. Start by saving at least $500, then work your way up to 3-6 months of expenses. This will give you the security to handle emergencies without going into debt.

Tip: *"I didn't have an emergency fund when my truck broke down, and it cost me big time. Even if you can only save a little each month, it adds up fast, and you'll thank yourself when life inevitably throws you a curveball."*

4. Prioritize Retirement, Even if It Feels Far Away

Retirement may seem like a lifetime away, especially when you're young and single. But the truth is, the earlier you start saving for retirement, the more you benefit from **compound**

interest. Even if you can only contribute a small percentage of your income, it's better than nothing. Start by contributing to your employer's 401(k) if available or open an IRA if you're self-employed or your job doesn't offer one.

Tip: *"I didn't take retirement seriously in my 20s, and now I'm playing catch-up. Don't be me. Start saving now and let compound interest do the work for you over time."*

5. Track Your Spending

It's easy to lose track of where your money goes, especially when you're juggling rent, utilities, groceries, and a social life. Use budgeting apps like **Mint**, **YNAB (You Need A Budget)**, or even a simple spreadsheet to track every dollar you spend. By keeping a close eye on your expenses, you can adjust where necessary and ensure that you're not overspending in any one category.

6. Build Good Credit

As a single person, your credit score is entirely your responsibility. Having good credit is crucial for renting apartments, securing loans, or even getting lower insurance rates. Here's how to build and maintain a good credit score:

- **Pay Your Bills on Time**: Set up automatic payments or reminders to ensure you never miss a due date.

- **Keep Your Credit Utilization Low**: Try to use no more than 30% of your available credit limit.

- **Check Your Credit Report Regularly**: Make sure there are no errors or signs of fraud. You can get a free credit report once a year from each of the three major credit bureaus.

Tip: *"A strong credit score opens a lot of doors, so treat it like gold. Pay on time, don't max out your cards, and check for any mistakes."*

7. Budget for Fun – Yes, You're Allowed to Enjoy Yourself!

Just because you're saving for the future doesn't mean you can't have fun in the present. Use the 30% portion of your budget for entertainment, dining out, travel, or whatever else brings you joy. The key is to enjoy yourself without going overboard. By planning for fun, you avoid the guilt of overspending and stay on track with your financial goals.

Tip: *"Budgeting isn't about cutting out all the fun. It's about being smart with your money so you can enjoy life now and in the future."*

CLOSING THOUGHTS: YOU'VE GOT THIS

Flying solo is the perfect time to get your financial act together. You don't have to worry about anyone else's money habits, and you have complete control over your finances. By building good financial habits now, automating your savings, and staying disciplined, you'll set yourself up for long-term success. And remember, you're allowed to enjoy your hard-earned money; just make sure you're planning for the future, too. You've got this!

CHECKLIST FOR SINGLES:

- Follow the 50/30/20 rule for budgeting.

- Automate savings for your emergency fund and retirement.

- Track spending using a budgeting app or spreadsheet.

- Prioritize building good credit by paying bills on time and keeping debt low.

- Set up a system to avoid emotional spending (e.g., waiting 24 hours before making purchases).

- Build an emergency fund with 3-6 months of expenses.

- Enjoy your money but keep it within the 30% of your budget for fun.

22

Budget Like a Boss

Chapter 2

Budgeting for Married Couples

TWO INCOMES,)NE PLAN

Marriage isn't just a partnership in life; it's also a partnership in money. When you're sharing your life with someone, you're also sharing the responsibility of managing finances. Budgeting as a couple can be challenging because you're not only blending incomes but also financial habits, priorities, and even past financial decisions. This chapter is all about how to combine your finances smoothly, avoid money-related conflicts, and build a future together.

ANECDOTE:

LEARNING TO WORK TOGETHER

"When I was married for the first time back in the '90s, we didn't really talk about money much at the beginning. My wife and I had very different views on spending. She loved buying home décor, and I was all about spending money on my '67 Chevelle. It wasn't long before the arguments started, and we realized we had to get on the same page.

Once we sat down, built a budget together, and really talked about our priorities, things started to smooth out. The key to avoiding money conflicts is communication and compromise."

ACTION PLAN FOR COUPLES

Working together on your finances can strengthen your relationship and set you up for a successful financial future. Here's how to get started:

1. Set Up a Joint Account for Shared Expenses

While you and your spouse may each have individual spending habits, it's essential to have a system for shared expenses. A joint account can be a great tool for managing household costs like rent/mortgage, utilities, groceries, and family-related expenses. It simplifies things, so you're not constantly asking, "Who's paying for what?"

How to Use It: Both partners contribute a set percentage of their income to the joint account each month. This keeps things fair, especially if one person earns more than the other.

Tip: *"My wife and I set up a joint account for household expenses, and it took the guesswork out of budgeting. We both knew what we were contributing and where the money was going."*

2. Create a Household Budget Together

Sitting down together to create a budget is critical for

financial harmony. Start by listing all of your combined income and expenses. Be sure to cover:

- Housing costs
- Utilities
- Groceries
- Car payments and insurance
- Debt repayments
- Entertainment
- Savings for future goals (*vacation, emergency fund, home improvements*)

Discuss your shared goals, and make sure both partners feel like their priorities are represented in the budget.

Financial Date Night: Set aside time once a month to review the budget together. Make it enjoyable; have a glass of wine, relax, and talk about your financial progress. Regular check-ins help avoid future surprises and keep both of you on the same page.

Tip: *"Our first 'money talk' wasn't easy, but when we turned it into a monthly habit, it stopped being a point of tension. Instead, it became a regular check-in that kept us both informed and on track."*

3. Split Your Spending Money

One common point of friction in marriages is personal spending. The solution?

Each partner should have their own "fun money" to spend however they like, no questions asked. Decide on an amount that fits within your budget, and then you can each spend that money however you choose without feeling guilty or judged.

How It Works: After covering the essentials and savings, allocate a set amount to each person for discretionary spending. This gives both of you financial independence and prevents arguments over personal purchases.

Tip: *"Giving ourselves 'fun money' was a game changer for my wife and me. She didn't have to justify her new shoes, and I didn't have to explain my car upgrades. It kept things balanced."*

Aligning Financial Mindsets in a Relationship

One of the biggest challenges in marriage is that people often come into relationships with different financial mindsets. Maybe one partner is a spender and the other is a saver, or maybe one likes to take financial risks while the other prefers security. These differences can cause friction if not addressed early on.

Understanding Each Other's Financial Habits

Talk About Money Early and Often: It's crucial to understand each other's financial history and habits. Discuss things like how you each handled money growing up, any debt you might be bringing into the marriage, and your general attitudes toward saving, spending, and investing.

Set Common Goals: The easiest way to align your financial mindsets is to agree on shared goals. Whether it's buying a house, saving for retirement, or planning for kids, having mutual goals helps keep you both on track.

Compromise and Respect

Balance Each Other's Strengths: If one of you is more detail-oriented, that person can handle day-to-day budgeting. If the other is a big-picture thinker, they can focus on long-term financial planning. The key is to respect each other's strengths and weaknesses.

Compromise: There's no one right way to manage money in a relationship. The key is finding a system that works for both of you. Maybe the spender can have more control over smaller, discretionary purchases, while the saver focuses on building your emergency fund and long-term savings.

4. Automate Your Savings for Shared Goals

As a couple, you'll likely have shared financial goals—whether it's saving for a home, a vacation, or your future family. The best way to ensure you're consistently working toward these goals is to automate your savings.

How It Works: Set up automatic transfers from your joint account into a separate savings account earmarked for specific goals. Decide together how much you'll contribute each month, and let automation take care of the rest.

Tip: *"We set up an automatic transfer for our down payment fund, and honestly, I forgot about it most of the time. When we finally checked, we had saved more than we expected."*

5. Plan for the Unexpected Together

Life is unpredictable, and planning for emergencies is essential. Make sure you and your spouse are both on the same page about building an emergency fund. Aim for 3-6 months' worth of expenses in a savings account you can both access in case of job loss, medical emergencies, or unexpected repairs.

How to Start: Even if you can only save a small amount at first, prioritize building that emergency fund. Make it part of your automated savings plan.

Tip: *"Having an emergency fund saved us from a lot of stress when my wife lost her job. Knowing we had a cushion made a tough time much easier to handle."*

6. Talk About Long-Term Goals

Budgeting as a couple isn't just about the day-to-day expenses. It's also about planning for your future together. Discuss your long-term financial goals; retirement, buying a second home, or even traveling more and start saving for them now.

How It Works: Open a savings or investment account dedicated to your long-term goals. Work with a financial advisor if necessary to make sure you're on track.

Tip: *"We didn't talk about our long-term plans until later in our marriage, and it made things harder. Once we started planning for the future, budgeting became less of a chore and more about achieving our shared dreams."*

7. Seek Professional Help for Big Financial Decisions

When it comes to major financial decisions, like buying a home, investing, or starting a family, it's a good idea to get professional advice. A financial advisor can help you create a roadmap that works for both of you and avoid costly mistakes.

Why It Matters: A neutral third party can help guide your conversations, especially if you and your spouse have different opinions about how to handle big financial decisions. They can also offer insight into tax strategies, retirement planning, and other complex financial matters.

Tip: *"We waited too long to talk to a financial advisor. When we finally did, it cleared up so many questions we had about our finances and helped us avoid mistakes."*

CLOSING THOUGHTS: YOU'RE IN THIS TOGETHER

Budgeting as a couple can seem like a daunting task, but it doesn't have to be a source of conflict. By working together, communicating openly, and setting shared goals, you can build a financial future that supports both of you. Remember, the key is teamwork; when you're both involved in the process, you're more likely to avoid the pitfalls of financial stress and build a stronger, more financially secure relationship.

YOU'VE GOT THIS, TOGETHER.

Checklist for Married Couples:

- Set up a joint account for shared expenses.

- Create a household budget together and schedule regular financial check-ins.

- Allocate personal spending money for each partner to avoid arguments over discretionary purchases.

- Align your financial mindsets through communication and compromise.

- Automate savings for your shared financial goals (e.g.,

buying a home or saving for a vacation).

- Build an emergency fund for 3-6 months' worth of expenses.

- Discuss long-term goals like retirement and start saving early.

- Seek professional advice for big financial decisions.

31

Chapter 3

Budgeting for Families

MORE PEOPLE, MORE EXPENSES

When you're budgeting for a family, the stakes get higher. You're no longer just responsible for your own needs; you're managing the finances for an entire household, which likely includes kids, school supplies, groceries, and family activities. But don't worry, managing a family budget doesn't have to be overwhelming. With the right plan in place, you can keep your family's finances organized, save for the future, and still have room for fun.

ANECDOTE

JUGGLING FAMILY EXPENSES

When I got remarried in 2002 and we started raising a family, the bills just kept piling up. Between the school supplies, birthday parties, clothes, and braces; there was always something that needed paying for. It felt like we were constantly playing catch-up. It wasn't until we sat down and built a solid budget that we could get ahead of it all.

Once we had a plan in place, we found room for not only the essentials but also for the things we wanted as a family, like vacations and saving for the kids' future. Budgeting made everything more manageable."

ACTION PLAN FOR FAMILIES

Budgeting for a family may seem complex, but with a few key strategies, you can manage both daily expenses and long-term goals.

1. Prioritize Necessities

When managing a family's finances, the first step is to cover your essentials.

These include:

- **Housing**: Rent or mortgage, utilities

- **Food**: Groceries, meal planning

- **Health**: Medical bills, insurance premiums, and prescriptions

- **Education**: School fees, supplies, and extracurricular activities

By focusing on these essential categories first, you ensure that your family is always provided for, no matter what else comes up.

Pro Tip: Plan meals ahead of time and buy groceries in bulk to reduce food costs. Meal prepping can also help avoid the temptation of takeout, which can quickly eat into your budget.

Tip: *"We used to spend so much on groceries because we weren't planning meals ahead. Once we started meal planning and buying in bulk, our grocery bill went way down, and we had more control over our food expenses."*

2. Set Aside Money for Family Goals

Every family has goals—whether it's saving for a vacation, a new home, or the kids' education. The trick is to set aside money for these goals little by little, so you're not scrambling to find the funds when the time comes.

How It Works: Create separate savings accounts for each goal (vacation, education fund, emergency fund), and automate transfers from your main account to each of these goals. Even if you're only saving a small amount each month, it will add up over time.

Tip: *"We always wanted to take a big family vacation, but it seemed impossible with all the expenses. Once we started saving $50 here and $100 there each month, we had enough for that trip without stressing about the money."*

3. Use Budgeting Apps to Stay Organized

Managing a family's budget means tracking a lot of moving parts—groceries, bills, school fees, extracurricular activities, and more. Budgeting apps like **Mint**, **YNAB**, or **EveryDollar** can make this easier by helping you organize and categorize expenses. These apps can also send you reminders for bills and help you avoid missing any payments.

Pro Tip: Look for apps that allow you to set specific family-related goals, like savings for college or a vacation, and track your progress toward these goals.

Tip: "We started using an app to track our family budget, and it made a world of difference. Instead of wondering where the money went at the end of the month, we knew exactly where every dollar was going."

4. Plan for the Unexpected

Life with a family is unpredictable kids get sick, the car breaks down, or unexpected repairs pop up at home. This is why having an **emergency fund** is so important. Aim to save 3-6 months' worth of expenses to cover any financial surprises that come your way.

How to Build It: Start small by saving a few hundred dollars, then work your way up. Automate your savings, so you don't have to think about it, and keep this money in a separate account that's easily accessible.

Tip: "The emergency fund saved us more times than I can count. Having that cushion made it so we didn't have to stress every time an unexpected bill came in."

5. Get the Kids Involved in the Budget

Teaching your kids about money early on will set them up for financial success later in life. It also helps them understand the value of a dollar and why certain things; like family vacations; require saving. Involving them in the family budget can be as simple as showing them how to save for a toy they want or how to make smart spending choices.

Fun Idea: Create a "family fun" jar where everyone contributes a little each week toward a fun family activity. This not only teaches kids about saving but also shows them how to work toward a common goal.

Tip: *"We started having our kids save for the things they wanted, and it completely changed how they looked at money. Now they know that not everything comes for free— and they appreciate what they save for."*

MANAGING FINANCES
BLENDED OR EXTENDED FAMILIES

Blended families or extended households often have more complex financial dynamics. Whether you're navigating child support, merging finances from previous marriages, or sharing expenses with other family members, budgeting can get tricky. Here's how to keep things organized in these situations:

Combining Finances from Previous Relationships

In blended families, each partner may bring their own financial history to the table, including debt, child support, or separate savings goals. It's essential to have open and honest conversations about how you'll manage these different financial responsibilities.

How to Manage It: Set up a joint account for shared family expenses like housing, groceries, and utilities, while keeping individual accounts for personal expenses or obligations like child support.

Tip: *"When my wife and I blended our finances, we had to be clear about who was responsible for what. It took some time, but once we had a system in place, everything ran more smoothly."*

BUDGETING FOR EXTENDED FAMILIES
MULTI-GENERATIONAL HOUSEHOLDS

If you're supporting extended family members or living in a

multi-generational household, it's important to factor in those additional costs. Whether it's helping with your parents' medical bills or supporting an adult child, clear boundaries and open communication are key.

Pro Tip: Create a specific category in your budget for extended family expenses, so you can track how much you're contributing and adjust as necessary.

Plan for Big Family Milestones

Major life events like sending kids to college, buying a home, or planning a wedding can put significant pressure on your budget. It's important to plan for these milestones in advance so that you're not caught off guard when the time comes.

How to Prepare: Start a **529 College Savings Plan** for your kids as early as possible, so their education fund grows over time. For other milestones, set up dedicated savings accounts and automate contributions toward those goals.

Tip: *"We started saving for our kids' college education early, and even though we didn't have a lot to put away at first, it grew over time. By the time they were ready for school, we were in a much better financial position."*

Have Fun Without Breaking the Bank

Raising a family doesn't mean you can't have fun; but it does mean finding affordable ways to do it. Instead of splurging on expensive vacations or activities, look for free or low-cost options like local parks, family game nights, or community events.

Pro Tip: Set a monthly entertainment budget and make it a family goal to find creative ways to stay within that limit. This can be a fun challenge that teaches kids the value of money while still making great family memories.

Tip: *"Some of the best memories we've made as a family didn't cost much at all. Camping trips, beach days, or even just movie nights at home; what matters is the time you spend together, not how much you spend."*

CLOSING THOUGHTS: ORGANIZE, PLAN, AND ENJOY

Budgeting for a family can feel like juggling a million things at once, but with the right plan in place, it's absolutely manageable. Prioritize your necessities, set aside money for the future, and don't forget to have some fun along the way. The earlier you start saving for big family goals; like education or vacations, the easier it will be to reach them. And remember, you don't have to do it all at once. Small, consistent steps will get you where you need to be. You've got this!

CHECKLIST FOR FAMILIES:

- Prioritize essential expenses like housing, food, and health.

- Set aside money for long-term family goals (education, vacations, emergency fund).

- Use budgeting apps to track multiple categories and stay organized.

- Build an emergency fund to cover 3-6 months' worth of living expenses.

- Involve your kids in the budgeting process to teach them about money management.

- Plan for big family milestones early, like college or

home buying.

Enjoy affordable family activities and make memories without overspending.

42

Chapter 4

Budgeting for Single Mothers
EVERY DOLLAR COUNTS

Being a single mother is one of the most challenging financial roles. You're' not just managing your own finances; you're responsible for the well-being of your children, and every dollar must stretch further. This chapter is designed to help single mothers create a budget that covers essential expenses, finds resources for additional support, and builds a financially secure future for both themselves and their children.

ANECDOTE:
SEEING MY SISTER DO IT ALL

"My sister raised three kids on her own after her husband passed away. She worked two jobs to make ends meet and was constantly juggling bills, meals, and finding time for her kids. But she made it work; barely. It wasn't until I sat down with her and we looked over her finances that she realized she needed a better system.

Once she set up a budget and started using some of the programs available to single parents, her life got a little easier. It's not easy, but with a good plan, you can make it work."

ACTION PLAN FOR SINGLE MOTHERS

As a single mother, you're wearing multiple hats, and it can feel overwhelming. But with a solid plan and the right resources, you can take control of your finances and provide for your family.

1. Cover the Essentials First

When budgeting with a single income, the first priority is to cover the essentials.

These include:

- **Housing**: Rent or mortgage, utilities

- **Food**: Groceries, meal planning

- **Transportation**: Car payments, insurance, and fuel or public transportation costs

- **Childcare**: Daycare, school fees, or babysitting

By focusing on these core expenses first, you ensure that the basic needs of you and your children are met. Any remaining funds can be allocated to savings or discretionary spending.

Pro Tip: Plan meals in advance and shop in bulk to save on groceries. Single mothers often face time constraints, so meal prepping can help reduce both time and costs.

Tip: *"My sister used to buy groceries on a whim, and it drained her budget fast. Once she started meal planning* *and buying in bulk, her grocery bill went down, and she had more control over her spending."*

2. Build an Emergency Fund, Even If It's Small

As a single parent, financial emergencies can hit hard, and without another income to rely on, it's critical to have an emergency fund in place. Start small; aim for at least $500 to cover basic emergencies like car repairs or medical bills. Over time, work toward building an emergency fund that covers 3-6 months' worth of living expenses.

How to Start: Save a little from each paycheck, even if it's only $20. Automating these savings into a separate account ensures you're building a financial safety net for your family.

Tip: *"It's tough to save on a single income, but even small amounts add up. My sister started with $10 a week, and before she knew it, she had enough saved to cover a car repair without stressing."*

3. Prioritize Debt Repayment

Many single mothers are dealing with debt, whether from credit cards, medical bills, or student loans. High-interest debt can quickly eat away at your income, so it's essential to make debt repayment a priority.

How to Manage It: Focus on paying off high-interest debt first. Consider using the **debt snowball method** (paying off the smallest debt first for quick wins) or the **debt avalanche method** (paying off the highest-interest debt first to save more in the long run). Whichever method you choose, consistency is key.

Tip: *"My sister was drowning in credit card debt, and it seemed impossible to get ahead. We sat down and came up* *with a plan to tackle the high-interest debt first, and slowly but surely, she started to see progress."*

4. Find Assistance Programs

There are many government and community resources available to single mothers that can help ease the financial burden. These programs can provide assistance with housing, food, healthcare, and childcare.

Key Programs: Look into **SNAP** (Supplemental Nutrition Assistance Program) for food, **WIC** (Women, Infants, and Children) for nutritional assistance, and **Section 8 Housing** for affordable housing options. You can also explore local charities or community groups that offer help with childcare or utilities.

Tip: *"My sister didn't realize there were so many programs out there to help single parents. Once she started using these resources, it took a lot of the pressure off."*

EMERGENCY FINANCIAL PLANNING
FOR SINGLE PARENTS

As a single mother, the financial impact of emergencies can be devastating. Whether it's a job loss, a medical emergency, or unexpected home repairs, it's important to have a plan in place for handling these situations.

1. Start a Basic Emergency Fund

Even if you can only save a small amount, having something set aside for emergencies is critical. Start by setting aside whatever you can, whether it's $5 or $50 per paycheck. The key is to build up that cushion over time so that you're not left scrambling when something unexpected happens.

2. Know Your Backup Options

If you face a financial emergency and your savings aren't enough, have a plan for how you'll get additional help. This might include:

- Borrowing from family or friends (with a repayment plan in place)

- Using community resources or food banks

- Seeking a small personal loan with low interest

- Contacting creditors to negotiate payment plans in case of job loss or illness

3. Keep Emergency Essentials Ready

While an emergency fund is crucial, there are other ways to prepare for emergencies. Stock up on essential items like non-perishable food, basic medical supplies, and household necessities. This way, if your budget is tight due to an emergency, you won't have to worry about these critical expenses.

FINANCIAL RESOURCES
LOW-INCOME SINGLE PARENTS

Many single mothers find themselves managing finances on a tight budget. Fortunately, there are a number of programs designed to help low-income parents cover the essentials and save for the future.

1. Government Assistance Programs

- **TANF** (*Temporary Assistance for Needy Families*): Provides temporary financial assistance to help cover living expenses.

- **Medicaid**: Offers healthcare coverage for low-income families.

- **Childcare Assistance Programs**: Many states offer subsidized childcare programs to help single mothers afford daycare.

2. Educational Grants and Scholarships

If you're a single mother looking to further your education, there are grants and scholarships available specifically for single parents. These can help cover tuition, books, and other school-related expenses, making it easier to pursue your career goals.

- **Pell Grants**: Available to low-income individuals pursuing higher education.

- **Single Parent Scholarships**: Many colleges and organizations offer scholarships specifically for single parents. Be sure to research options in your state or through nonprofit organizations.

3. Local Community Support

Don't overlook local resources. Many communities have nonprofit organizations, churches, and food banks that offer support for single mothers. Whether it's help with groceries, free financial counseling, or assistance with utility bills, these local programs can make a big difference.

Tip: *"My sister found a local food bank that helped her get through some really tight months. Sometimes, it's the community around you that provides the most support."*

4. Focus on Your Long-Term Goals

Even though immediate needs can seem overwhelming,

it's important to plan for the future. Setting long-term goals, like building savings for your children's education or eventually buying a home, can help keep you motivated.

How to Save: Start by contributing small amounts to a **529 College Savings Plan** or setting aside a small portion of your income for a future down payment on a home. Even if you're only saving a little, it will add up over time and give you something to build on.

Tip: *"It's tough when you're living paycheck to paycheck, but having a long-term goal helps keep you focused. My sister started small, saving just $10 a month for her kids' college, and now she's amazed at how much it's grown."*

5. Seek Out Financial Education

One of the best investments you can make is in your financial knowledge. Many organizations offer free financial education classes or counseling services that can help you manage your money more effectively.

Where to Find Help: Look for local community centers or nonprofits that offer financial literacy programs. Many online resources and webinars are also available for free, covering topics like budgeting, saving, and debt management.

CLOSING THOUGHTS:
YOU ARE STRONGER THAN YOU THINK

Being a single mother is no easy task, but with the right plan, resources, and mindset, you can manage your finances successfully and build a bright future for your family. Start by covering the basics, finding assistance where needed, and setting small goals to help you move forward. Remember, every little bit counts, and with time and discipline, you can achieve financial security. You've got this!

CHECKLIST FOR SINGLE MOTHERS:

- Prioritize essential expenses: housing, food, childcare, and transportation.

- Start building an emergency fund, even if it's just $20 per paycheck.

- Tackle high-interest debt using the snowball or avalanche method.

- Research and apply for government assistance programs (SNAP, TANF, Medicaid).

- Consider opening a 529 plan or savings account for your children's education.

- Find free or low-cost financial education resources to boost your money management skills.

- Prepare a backup plan for emergencies, including knowing where to find community support.

51

Chapter 5

Budgeting After Divorce

STARTING OVER

Divorce can be emotionally and financially overwhelming. After the separation, you're left to rebuild your life and your finances, often with significant changes in income, expenses, and priorities. While it's a challenging time, it's also an opportunity to create a new financial foundation. This chapter is dedicated to helping you navigate the financial side of life after divorce, from managing debt to planning for your future.

ANECDOTE:

MY OWN FINANCIAL REBUILD

"When I went through my divorce, I had no idea what I was in for financially. Between legal fees, splitting up assets, and her moving out of the house, I was in a tight spot for a while. It felt like starting from scratch. I had to rebuild my finances brick by brick, starting with paying off the debts I took on after the separation. It was tough, but I came out the other side with a stronger understanding of money management. Divorce might knock you down, but it's also an opportunity to start fresh."

ACTION PLAN
FOR REBUILDING AFTER DIVORCE:

Post-divorce finances can feel like a jigsaw puzzle, but by taking things one step at a time, you can regain control and rebuild your financial life.

1. Start with a New Budget

Your financial situation has likely changed significantly after the divorce. Whether you're adjusting to a lower income, paying child support or alimony, or managing higher living expenses on your own, it's crucial to create a new budget that reflects your current situation.

How to Do It: Start by listing your new income and all of your expenses, including rent, utilities, child-related costs, and any debts. Be realistic about what you can afford and where you might need to make cuts.

Your new budget should focus on covering the essentials first; housing, food, and transportation, while slowly building back your savings.

Tip: *"After my divorce, I had to rethink everything. My expenses were higher because I was on my own again, but my income hadn't changed. The first thing I did was create a budget that fit my new reality, which helped me avoid falling further into debt."*

2. Prioritize Debt Repayment

Divorce often comes with debt; whether it's legal fees, splitting credit card balances, or paying off joint loans. Tackling this debt head-on should be a priority. The last thing you want is for high-interest debt to drag you down as you're trying to start over.

How to Manage It: Use the **debt snowball** or **debt avalanche** method to chip away at your post-divorce debt. The snowball method focuses on paying off the smallest debt first for a quick win, while the avalanche method targets high-interest debt first to save money over time.

Tip: *"I had to deal with a lot of debt after my divorce, but I made a plan to pay off the highest-interest debt first. Little by little, I started to get ahead, and it felt great to see my debt go down."*

3. Adjust to a New Financial Reality

One of the hardest adjustments after divorce is learning to live on a single income or dealing with financial obligations like child support or alimony. It's crucial to reassess your financial goals and prioritize saving for your new life. This is a good time to re-frame your expectations and focus on the long-term.

How to Do It: Take a hard look at your spending habits and adjust them to fit your new income. You may need to downsize your living situation, cut unnecessary expenses, or delay large purchases. Focus on building a secure financial foundation before making any major financial commitments.

Tip: *"After my divorce, I had to downsize. It wasn't easy, but it gave me the breathing room I needed to get back on track. Sometimes, starting fresh means making tough decisions in the short term to ensure a stable future."*

4. Build an Emergency Fund

It's crucial to have a financial safety net, especially post-divorce. While you may have tapped into your savings during the divorce process, now is the time to start rebuilding. Aim for at least 3-6 months' worth of living expenses in an emergency fund to protect yourself from future financial crises.

How to Rebuild: Start small and automate your savings. Even setting aside $20 from each paycheck can make a difference over time. Keep this money in a separate, easily accessible account.

Tip: *"I had to drain most of my savings during the divorce, but rebuilding my emergency fund became my top priority afterward. Having that safety net in place was a huge relief and gave me peace of mind."*

5. Focus on Your Long-Term Goals

It's important to set new financial goals after divorce. Whether it's buying a new home, saving for retirement, or planning for your children's future, having long-term goals gives you something to work toward.

How to Do It: Start by identifying one or two key goals, like saving for a down payment on a home or building up your retirement fund. Break these goals into smaller, manageable steps, and track your progress. If you received a portion of retirement assets in the divorce settlement, make sure you understand the tax implications and how to reinvest that money for your future.

Tip: *"After the dust settled, I realized I had to start thinking about my future again. I set a few big goals; like buying my own home and rebuilding my retirement fund and focused on those, one step at a time."*

NAVIGATING FINANCIAL CRISES POST-DIVORCE

Divorce can trigger a financial crisis, especially if you were financially dependent on your spouse or if the divorce was unexpected. It's important to know how to navigate financial emergencies after the divorce is finalized.

1. Understand Your New Financial Situation

Take a close look at your new financial landscape. This includes knowing exactly what debts you're responsible for, how much income you're bringing in, and what financial commitments (such as child support or alimony) you'll need to manage.

2. Create a Crisis Budget

In times of financial uncertainty, it's essential to have a crisis budget in place. This is a bare-bones version of your budget that focuses only on covering the essentials; housing, food, utilities, and transportation. Cut back on non-essential spending until your financial situation stabilizes.

3. Seek Professional Financial Advice

If you're feeling overwhelmed by your financial situation post-divorce, consider seeking help from a financial advisor. They can help you make sense of your new circumstances and create a plan to get back on track. A financial advisor can also help you reinvest any assets received from the divorce settlement and manage any tax implications.

4. Rebuild Your Credit

Divorce can take a toll on your credit score, especially if joint debts weren't handled well during the separation. Rebuilding your credit should be a priority, as good credit is essential for renting a home, securing a loan, or even getting a job.

How to Do It: Check your credit report for any errors or joint accounts that need to be closed. Focus on paying your bills on time and keeping your credit utilization low. Consider using a secured credit card if necessary to rebuild your credit score.

Tip: *"After the divorce, my credit score took a hit. It took some time, but by paying my bills on time and keeping my debt low, I was able to rebuild my credit."*

5. Take Care of Your Mental Health

Divorce is emotionally draining, and the financial stress only adds to the burden. It's important to take care of your mental health during this time. Seek support from friends, family, or a therapist if needed. Financial stress can be overwhelming, but taking care of your mental well-being will help you stay focused on rebuilding your life.

CLOSING THOUGHTS: A NEW BEGINNING

Divorce is one of life's most challenging transitions, but it's also a chance to start fresh. By creating a new budget, tackling your debt, and setting new financial goals, you can rebuild your financial life and create a secure future for yourself. Remember, the key is to take things one step at a time and not to get overwhelmed. You've got this, and the future is full of new possibilities.

CHECKLIST FOR BUDGETING AFTER DIVORCE:

- Create a new budget that reflects your current financial reality.

- Prioritize paying off debt, focusing on high-interest debt first.

- Build an emergency fund, even if you can only save a small amount at first.

- Set new long-term financial goals and work toward them gradually.

- Rebuild your credit score by paying bills on time and managing debt.

- Seek financial advice to help you navigate complex financial decisions and assets from the divorce.

- Take care of your mental health during this challenging transition.

Chapter 6

Budgeting for Retirement
PLANNING FOR THE GOLDEN YEARS

Congratulations! You've worked hard, and now retirement is on the horizon, or maybe you're already enjoying it. Retirement is a time to relax, travel, and finally check off those bucket list items; whether it's a road trip across the country, learning how to paint, or just perfecting your golf swing. But before you can sit back and sip lemonade on your front porch, you need to make sure your finances are in order. here to guide you through budgeting for your golden years, with a bit of humor and a lot of practical advice.

ANECDOTE:
THE EARLY RETIREMENT DREAM (AND REALITY)

"You know, back when I was in my 30s, I thought I'd be living the dream by 50; retired, fishing every day, maybe even owning a beach house. Well, fast forward to 50, and I was still working six days a week at my towing business, wondering how on earth I'd ever be able to afford retirement.

Spoiler alert: the beach house didn't happen.

But what did happen was I got smart with my money in my 50s, started saving like my life depended on it (which, by the way, it kind of does in retirement), and I'm now living pretty comfortably in my retirement; though I'm still waiting on that fishing boat. The key? Planning early and being realistic about what retirement looks like."

ACTION PLAN FOR RETIREMENT:

Whether you're retiring with a partner or enjoying your golden years solo, you'll want to plan carefully to make your money last. Here's how to budget smart for retirement.

1. Estimate Your Retirement Expenses

The first step in building your retirement budget is figuring out how much you'll need to cover your expenses once you're no longer working. Spoiler alert: it's probably more than you think. You might not be commuting to work anymore, but there are plenty of other costs to consider.

How to Do It: Write down your anticipated monthly expenses, including housing, groceries, healthcare, utilities, and any hobbies you plan to indulge in (finally getting that woodworking shop or taking up golf; fair warning, both can get expensive fast).

Tip: *"Don't make the mistake I did and assume your spending will drop just because you're retired. My grocery bill went up, not down, thanks to all the free time I suddenly had to start gourmet cooking. Let's just say, the price of truffle oil adds up."*

2. Social Security: Maximize Your Benefits

If you're like most retirees, Social Security will be a big part of your income. But don't rush to start collecting the moment you hit 62. The longer you wait, the bigger your check will be. If you can hold out until age 70, you'll get the maximum benefit.

How to Do It: Sit down and crunch the numbers. If you start taking Social Security early (at 62), you'll get smaller monthly checks for the rest of your life. But if you can wait until full retirement age (67 for most of us), or even better, until 70, those checks get bigger.

 Tip: *"I thought I was going to start collecting Social Security the second I turned 62, but my accountant practically tackled me to stop me. 'Wait, Aaron!' she yelled, 'You'll get more money if you hold off!' Turns out, she was right. Sometimes waiting pays off... literally."*

3. Plan for Healthcare Costs

Healthcare is one of the biggest expenses retirees face. Even if you're in great shape now, Medicare doesn't cover everything, and medical costs can pile up quickly as you age. Prescription drugs, dental care, vision; it all adds up, and if you're not ready for it, it can blow a hole in your budget faster than a flat tire on the freeway.

How to Do It: Make sure to budget for Medicare premiums, supplemental insurance, and out-of-pocket expenses. Consider a **Health Savings Account (HSA)** if you're still working, as it allows you to save tax-free money for medical expenses in retirement.

 Tip: *"Look, I thought I'd be one of those guys still running marathons at 70, but instead I've got a medicine cabinet that looks like a mini pharmacy. Between the heartburn meds, cholesterol pills, and my 'Don't even ask what that's for' pre-scription, healthcare costs are no joke. Plan for it."*

RETIREMENT TOGETHER
DOUBLE THE FUN (AND THE EXPENSES)

If you're retiring with your partner, things can get a little trickier. On the one hand, you've got two Social Security checks coming in (yay!). On the other hand, you've also got double the expenses (oh, no). You'll need to coordinate your finances carefully to make sure you're both on the same page, and don't forget to plan for one partner potentially outliving the other (not the most fun conversation, but necessary).

1. Combine Your Retirement Savings

If you and your spouse have separate retirement accounts, now's the time to look at them together. How much do you have saved, and how long will it last? Make sure you're working toward the same goals, whether that's traveling the world or just relaxing at home.

How to Do It: Sit down with your partner and review your combined assets. Create a joint budget that accounts for both of your incomes and expected expenses.

Tip: *"When my second wife and talked about retirement, we sat down to combine our savings, and she said, 'Wait, you've been spending all our retirement money on car parts?!' Lesson learned: talk to your partner about finances BEFORE you retire."*

2. Plan for One Spouse Outliving the Other

As tough as it is to think about, chances are one of you will outlive the other. Make sure you've planned for that financially, especially if one of you is more financially dependent on the other's income. Look into survivor benefits for Social Security and pensions.

Tip: *"This one isn't fun to think about, but it's important. My buddy George didn't plan for his wife to outlive him, and now she's living off his Social Security checks alone. Don't let that happen to your family, plan ahead."*

RETIREMENT ALONE
THE SOLO JOURNEY

For those flying solo in retirement, the good news is that you've only got one person to worry about. The bad news? Well, it's still just you managing everything, and that can feel overwhelming. But with a little planning, you can enjoy your solo retirement without any financial hiccups.

1. Stretching Your Savings

When you're single in retirement, your savings need to go the extra mile. It's important to be realistic about how long your money will last and how much you'll need for the lifestyle you want.

How to Do It: Calculate your annual expenses, then figure out how much you can safely withdraw from your savings each year. Most experts recommend the **4% rule**, which suggests withdrawing no more than 4% of your savings each year to make sure it lasts.

Tip: *"After my second divorce, I realized it was just me and my savings. It was a little terrifying at first, but I made sure to stretch every dollar like it was a piece of gum. You'd be* *amazed at how far you can make your money go if you plan carefully."*

2. Maximize Social Security

Just like with couples, it's important to make the most of your Social Security benefits when you're on your own. Waiting to claim until age 70 can significantly increase your monthly checks, which is a big help when you're only relying on one income stream.

4. Downsizing: Less Can Be More

Retirement is the perfect time to simplify your life. Do you really need that big house now that the kids are gone? Downsizing can free up a lot of money, reduce maintenance, and lower your living costs.

How to Do It: Consider selling your home and moving into something smaller. Or, if you're not ready to give up the house, think about renting out a room or two for extra income. You can also investigate moving to a more affordable area where the cost of living is lower.

Tip: *"John held onto his big ol' house for way too long after the kids moved out. It wasn't until he downsized that he realized, 'Hey, less house, less stress!' Plus, now he has extra cash for those fishing trips he's been dreaming about."*

5. Plan for Fun: Yes, You Can Enjoy Your Money

Retirement shouldn't be all about pinching pennies. You've worked hard for this, and it's time to enjoy the fruits of your labor. Whether that's traveling, taking up a new hobby, or just spending time with the grandkids, make sure to budget for the fun stuff, too.

How to Do It: Set aside a portion of your retirement savings specifically for leisure and hobbies. Just be sure to track your spending, so you don't go overboard.

Tip: *"I may not have the beach house, but I do have a golf membership and a yearly fishing trip with the guys. Retirements about balance, enjoy yourself, but don't blow it all on one fancy vacation. Unless it's to Hawaii... then maybe it's worth it."*

CLOSING THOUGHTS
GOLDEN YEARS, GOLDEN OPPORTUNITIES

Retirement is your time to shine, but to make the most of it, you've got to plan smartly. From managing your savings to making the most of Social Security, every decision counts. But don't stress too much; retirement is supposed to be fun, after all! So, budget wisely, plan for the future, and most importantly, enjoy the ride. You've earned it!

CHECKLIST FOR RETIREMENT:

- Estimate your retirement expenses and create a realistic budget.

- Maximize your Social Security benefits by waiting to claim if possible.

- Plan for healthcare costs and consider a Health Savings Account (HSA).

- If retiring with a partner, combine finances and plan for one spouse outliving the other.

- If retiring alone, stretch your savings and downsize if necessary.

- Set aside money for fun; retirement is meant to be enjoyed!

69

Chapter 7

Retirement Alone

THE SOLO JOURNEY

So, you've made it to retirement on your own, huh? Maybe you're single, maybe the spouse ran off with the cabana boy, or maybe you've always been a lone wolf. Whatever the reason, the good news is that in retirement, you only have yourself to worry about! You don't have to argue over whether to buy the giant flat-screen TV or save for that European cruise (hint: you can do both if you plan right!). But it also means you're the only one managing everything; yep, it's all on you, buddy. Lucky for you, been through it, and he's here to help you figure out how to budget for a happy, solo retirement.

ANECDOTE:

GOING IT ALONE (AND LOVING IT)

"After my second divorce, I found myself on my own in

medical related retirement, and I gotta tell ya, there are perks. No more fighting over the thermostat, no more worrying about how much someone else's online shopping habit is costing us. But I also learned that it's a lot easier to manage your money when you're the only one spending it, until I found myself dangerously close to buying a hot tub with half my savings.

So, here's my advice: plan carefully, budget smart, and yes, leave a little room for fun; just maybe skip the impulse hot tub purchase."

ACTION PLAN FOR SOLO RETIREMENT

When you're on your own in retirement, you've got all the freedom; but also all the responsibility. The good news is you get to call the shots. Here's how to make sure you don't run out of money while living your best retired life.

1. Stretch Your Savings Like a Rubber Band

When you're retired and single, your savings need to go the extra mile; kinda like that elastic waistband in your sweatpants after Thanksgiving dinner. You might not have a second income stream coming in, so it's all about making what you've saved last for the long haul.

How to Do It: Use the **4% rule**. It's the golden rule for retirees, meaning you withdraw no more than 4% of your savings each year. This way, your nest egg doesn't run out faster than my patience when I see teenagers walking around with $8 coffee drinks.

Tip: *"I thought I could just dip into my savings whenever I wanted, like a kid in a candy store. Turns out, if you eat all the candy right away, you're left with an empty jar, and a stomachache. Pace yourself!"*

2. Maximize Your Social Security

When it comes to Social Security, patience is your best friend. Sure, you could start collecting at 62, but if you can wait until 70, those checks are going to be fatter than the stack of bills I used to get after taking the kids to Disneyland.

How to Do It: Delay claiming Social Security as long as you can. Every year you wait until full retirement age (67 for most of us) means a bigger check each month. Trust me, in the future you will thank present you for holding out.

Tip: *"I was itching to start collecting the minute I hit 62, but my financial advisor told me to sit tight. I waited until 70, and now I get to walk into IHOP, order the Grand Slam breakfast, and still have cash left over for dessert!"*

3. Downsizing: Less House, More Cash

If you're retired and on your own, do you really need that four-bedroom house with the backyard big enough to host the neighborhood BBQ? Downsizing is a smart way to free up some extra cash, lower your bills, and avoid cleaning a house big enough to get lost in.

How to Do It: Sell your big ol' house and move into something more manageable. Or, if you love your place too much to part with it, consider renting out a room for some extra income (just maybe avoid renting it to your cousin Larry, unless you want your place turned into a makeshift rock band rehearsal studio).

Tip: *A friend Frank said to me: "I held onto my big house way longer than I should've. One day, I was vacuuming the upstairs guest room (that no one had stayed in for five years), and I thought, 'Why am I doing this to myself?' I sold the place, got a cozy condo, and now I have extra money for* *the important things - like fishing gear and a really nice recliner."*

4. Plan for Fun: This Is YOUR Time

Retirement isn't just about saving and cutting costs; it's your time to have fun! Whether it's traveling, picking up a hobby, or finally finishing that collection of vintage spoons (hey, no judgment), make sure you budget for some good times. The key is to plan for fun without blowing all your savings on one big splurge.

How to Do It: Set aside a portion of your budget specifically for leisure. Whether it's for vacations, hobbies, or even just regular nights out with friends, having a "fun fund" ensures you can enjoy life without dipping into your emergency stash.

Tip: "When I retired, I made the mistake of thinking I couldn't afford to do anything fun. But what's the point of retirement if you're not enjoying it? Just don't spend it all on one big trip to Vegas; unless you're good at blackjack... in which case, can I come?"

5. Plan for the Unexpected

I hate to break it to you, but life doesn't stop throwing curveballs just because you're retired. Health issues, home repairs, surprise bills; they can all still hit, and you need to be ready for them. That's why having an emergency fund is so important.

How to Do It: Keep at least 3-6 months' worth of living expenses in an emergency fund. And don't touch it unless you really need to! No, that new set of golf clubs doesn't count as an emergency (even if you insist, they'll improve your game).

Tip: "I dipped into my emergency fund once to buy a set of new Golf Clubs. Big mistake. Turns out, those clubs were more decorative than functional. Now I've got a bag full of pretty clubs and a promise to myself to only use that fund for real emergencies; like when my car's transmission decided to quit on me."

6. Stay Social (Even If You're On Your Own)

Just because you're retired and single doesn't mean you should become a hermit. Staying connected with friends, family, and your community is key to keeping your spirits up. Plus, it gives you an excuse to get out of the house and spend some of that fun money.

How to Do It: Budget for activities with friends, whether it's weekly lunches, group travel, or even just a regular coffee catch-up. Being social doesn't have to be expensive, but it does need to be part of your life.

Tip: *"I thought retirement meant I'd be happy just hanging out at home with my TV remote, but after a while, I started talking to the toaster. Now, I make a point to meet my buddies for coffee every week. It's cheaper than therapy, and I get some human interaction; win-win."*

CLOSING THOUGHTS
YOU'RE THE CAPTAIN OF YOUR RETIREMENT SHIP

Being on your own in retirement means you get to steer the ship, but it also means you've got to be smart with your budget, so you don't end up shipwrecked on "Broke Island." Plan ahead, keep your savings on track, and don't forget to have fun along the way.

Whether you're downsizing, maxing out your Social Security, or just enjoying the freedom of retirement, you've earned this time to live life your way. So, go ahead; buy the fishing rod, take that trip, just maybe hold off on the hot tub.

CHECKLIST FOR SOLO RETIREES:

- Stretch your savings using the 4% rule.

- Maximize your Social Security benefits by waiting to claim if possible.

- Consider downsizing to free up extra cash and reduce expenses.

- Set up a "fun fund" to enjoy life without blowing your budget..

- Keep 3-6 months' worth of expenses in an emergency fund; just in case.

- Stay social by budgeting for activities with friends and family.

- Most importantly, enjoy your retirement! You've earned it.

Retirement Alone

Chapter 8

Budgeting with a 401(k)

MAKING YOUR SAVINGS LAST

Alright, you've been diligently socking money away into that 401(k) for years; maybe even decades. Now comes the fun part: figuring out how to live off that money in retirement without running out. It's a delicate dance, but with a bit of planning and wisdom (and, okay, a few missteps I've made along the way), you'll be well on your way to making your 401(k) last as long as you do.

ANECDOTE:
THE 401(K) JIGSAW PUZZLE

"Let me tell you, when I first started dipping into my 401(k), I treated it like a slot machine. 'Need new tires? Take a little out. Want to upgrade the TV? Sure, let's cash out a bit more!' Then I got hit with some fees and taxes that made me spit out my coffee. Turns out, the government doesn't just let you take money out willy-nilly without wanting their cut. So here's what I learned the hard way: there's a right way and a wrong way to use your 401(k). You're about to learn the right way; because trust me, you don't want to be sipping that bitter coffee like I was."

ACTION PLAN
FOR MANAGING YOUR 401(K):

Your 401(k) is likely one of the biggest pieces of your retirement pie, so you need to handle it carefully. The key is to withdraw strategically so you don't outlive your savings (or end up with a tax bill that makes you cry).

1. Know Your 401(k) Withdrawal Rules

First things first: you can't just start yanking money out of your 401(k) whenever you feel like it. You need to wait until you're 59 ½ to avoid a 10% early withdrawal penalty (unless you like giving the IRS free money). Once you hit 72, you're required to start taking **Required Minimum Distributions (RMDs)**; basically, Uncle Sam wants his cut, and you're going to have to start withdrawing whether you like it or not.

How to Do It: Before you hit 72, plan out how much you'll withdraw each year. You can usually take out 4-5% annually without depleting your nest egg too quickly.

Tip: *"I had a buddy who didn't realize he had to start taking RMDs at 72. He thought he was being smart by letting it sit and grow, but then BAM—he got hit with a 50% penalty for not withdrawing on time. Fifty percent! That's like burning half your paycheck. Don't be that guy."*

2. Avoid the Tax Monster

Here's the thing nobody likes to talk about: taxes. Every time you withdraw from your 401(k), Uncle Sam's going to want his piece of the pie. It's important to know how much of your savings will be taxed and plan accordingly, so you don't get a nasty surprise when you file your taxes.

How to Do It: Work with a financial advisor to figure out the most tax-efficient way to withdraw your money. You may want to withdraw just enough each year to keep yourself in a lower tax bracket (because who wants to give more money to the government than they have to?).

 Tip: *"The first time I took out a chunk of cash from my 401(k), I didn't think about taxes. And then when tax season rolled around, I was like, 'Wait, why is this number so big?!' Turns out, I'd bumped myself into a higher tax bracket. Lesson learned: be strategic."*

3. Strategically Combine Your 401(k) with Other Income Sources

If you've got Social Security, a pension, or other retirement accounts, you'll want to make sure you're not pulling too much from your 401(k) too early. The idea is to balance your income streams so you can make your savings last. Think of your 401(k) as the "meat" of your retirement meal, while Social Security and other income sources are the side dishes. You don't want to overdo it on the meat before you finish the potatoes.

How to Do It: Start with Social Security (once you've maximized your benefits, of course; see Chapter 6 for more on that), then use your 401(k) to fill in any gaps. If you have other income sources, like a pension or rental income, use those first to preserve your 401(k) for later years.

 Tip: *"I used to dip into my 401(k) like it was my personal* *piggy bank, but once I realized I had other income sources, I started balancing things out. Now I'm living comfortably off my Veterans Benefits and my part-time consulting gig, while my 401(k) just hangs out, getting fatter for when I really need it."*

4. Don't Blow It All on Day One

I know, I know; it's tempting to finally splurge on that dream vacation or buy the boat you've always wanted. But before you take a massive chunk out of your 401(k) for a one-time splurge, remember this: that money has to last you for decades. If you blow through it too quickly, you might find yourself in a tighter spot later on.

How to Do It: Budget for those big splurges, but make sure they're part of your overall financial plan. Set aside a portion of your savings specifically for fun stuff, so you can enjoy yourself without raiding your retirement.

Tip: *"When I retired, I wanted to take the ultimate fishing trip; Alaska, the works. But after looking at the cost, I realized I'd have to pull a big chunk out of my 401(k). Instead, I found a budget-friendly trip closer to home and still had a blast. Plus, my savings didn't take a hit. Alaska can wait—maybe for my 80th birthday."*

5. Make Your Money Last: The 4% Rule

The **4% rule** is a classic retirement strategy that helps you avoid running out of money too soon. The idea is simple: you withdraw 4% of your 401(k) each year, and by doing so, you should be able to live comfortably while letting your remaining savings continue to grow. If your portfolio performs well, you might even be able to withdraw a little more; but don't get greedy!

How to Do It: If you've got $500,000 saved in your 401(k), you'd take out $20,000 the first year. Each year after that, you adjust for inflation. The trick is to stick to this plan and avoid the temptation to dip into your savings for big, non-essential purchases.

Tip: *"I was skeptical of the 4% rule at first; I mean, it sounds so simple, right? But after a couple of years of sticking to it, I realized it was keeping me on track. Now I don't have to worry about running out of money before I hit 90, and I still get to enjoy my daily coffee and occasional fishing trip."*

6. Roll Over If You're Still Working

Planning to keep working part-time in retirement (like yours truly)? If your employer offers a 401(k), keep contributing as long as you can. This can be a great way to boost your savings and delay withdrawing from your original 401(k). Plus, it can keep you mentally sharp and socially engaged; because who wants to spend all day talking to the cat?

How to Do It: If you're working at 72 or beyond, make sure you roll over any new 401(k) contributions into your current plan. This way, you're still building your savings while delaying withdrawals from your main 401(k).

Tip: *"I picked up some part-time consulting work in retirement, and guess what? I could still contribute to a new 401(k)! It felt like a bonus round; extra savings, extra security, and fewer worries about running out of cash down the line."*

CLOSING THOUGHTS: IT'S ALL ABOUT BALANCE

Your 401(k) is a powerful tool, but it's not the only piece of the puzzle. By managing your withdrawals carefully, balancing your income streams, and keeping an eye on taxes, you can make sure your retirement savings last as long as you do; maybe even longer. Just remember: a little planning now means more peace of mind (and more fun) later. So, enjoy your retirement; just don't blow it all on that dream boat the first year, okay?

CHECKLIST FOR MANAGING YOUR 401(K):

- Wait until at least age 59 ½ to avoid early withdrawal penalties.

- Start Required Minimum Distributions (RMDs) by age 72 to avoid a 50% penalty.

- Work with a financial advisor to minimize taxes on your withdrawals.

- Combine your 401(k) with Social Security and other income sources strategically.

- Stick to the 4% rule to make sure your savings last.

- If you're still working, contribute to a new 401(k) and roll it over into your existing plan.

- Don't blow your savings on one big splurge; pace yourself!

Chapter 9

Budgeting on Social Security
STRETCHING YOUR DOLLARS

Well, look at you! You've worked hard, and now you're ready to enjoy the benefits of **Social Security**; those magical checks that show up like clockwork, helping you cover your expenses without punching a clock anymore. But here's the catch: Social Security isn't a one-size-fits-all solution to your retirement. For most folks, it's not enough to cover all your expenses, but with a little bit of savvy budgeting (and, as always, some wisdom from Uncle Aaron), you can make those dollars stretch further than a rubber band at a county fair.

ANECDOTE:
THE SOCIAL SECURITY SHUFFLE

"When My Friend Mike first started getting those Social Security checks, he thought, 'This is it? This is supposed to be my golden ticket?' Let's just say it wasn't enough to fund his yacht dreams. But after a few months of figuring out how to make it work, he learned some tricks to keep the bills paid and even set aside a little fun money. And no, he didn't need to sell his collection of limited-edition Elvis plates; though he says he came close, (that would have broken his Grandmothers heart). Trust me, with the right approach, you can make Social Security work for you."

ACTION PLAN
FOR LIVING ON SOCIAL SECURITY

Social Security checks are great, but they don't exactly make you a millionaire overnight. If you're like most retirees, you'll need to plan carefully to make sure your expenses don't outrun your income. Let's dive into some smart strategies to make sure your golden years stay, well, golden.

1. Create a Rock-Solid Budget (And Stick to It)

Social Security puts you on a fixed income, which means every dollar must count. The best way to stay on top of your finances is to build a budget that covers your essentials, with a little bit of wiggle room for the fun stuff (because, hey, what's retirement without a little fun?).

How to Do It: Start by listing all your fixed expenses: housing, utilities, groceries, healthcare, and any debt payments. Then, figure out how much you'll have left for discretionary spending; whether that's hobbies, dining out, or the occasional splurge on something nice.

Tip: *"I tried to wing it for the first few months on Social Security, but then I found myself eating ramen noodles for dinner way too often. Lesson learned: a solid budget means more steak nights and fewer sad noodle dinners."*

2. Maximize Your Benefits

Believe it or not, there are ways to squeeze a little more juice out of your Social Security. Delaying your claim until age 70 (if you can swing it) is one of the best ways to ensure bigger checks. If you're already collecting, there are still ways to make sure you're not missing out on extra benefits, especially if you qualify for spousal or survivor benefits.

How to Do It: Check with Social Security to see if you qualify for any additional benefits. If your spouse is collecting more than you, you may be able to claim half of their benefits instead. And if your spouse has passed away, don't forget to check on survivor benefits; they're designed to help you get by without them.

Tip: *"I was happily collecting my Social Security until some-one told me I could be getting more thanks to my late wife's benefits. Turns out, they owed me a chunk of cash I didn't even know about! A few phone calls later, I had some extra income coming in; score one for Uncle Aaron."*

3. Cut Costs Like a Pro

Living on Social Security means you might have to cut back in some areas, but it doesn't have to feel like a sacrifice. The trick is to find ways to lower your expenses without lowering your quality of life. Whether it's downsizing, reducing your bills, or finding discounts, every little bit helps.

How to Do It: Look at areas where you can save. Can you downsize to a smaller home or apartment? Could you switch to a cheaper phone plan or bundle your services? Don't be afraid to ask about senior discounts; you'd be amazed how many places offer them. And when in doubt, thrift stores are your new best friend.

Tip: *"I used to laugh at veteran/senior discounts—thought* *they were for 'old folks.' Then one day, I tried it at the diner and got 10% off my breakfast. That's when I realized, 'Wait a minute... this is the life!' Now, I'm the king of discounts. If there's a way to save a buck, you can bet I'm asking for it."*

4. Embrace a Simple Lifestyle (With a Side of Fun)

You don't need to live like a monk just because you're on Social Security. In fact, retirement is a great time to explore hobbies, spend time with friends, and maybe even pick up something new—all without blowing your budget.

How to Do It: Look for low-cost or free activities that bring you joy. Maybe it's gardening, volunteering, or joining a local community group. Many places offer free classes or workshops for seniors, and local libraries are gold mines for free entertainment (movies, books, events; you name it).

Tip: *"I used to think I needed money to have fun. Then I discovered my local senior center; these folks know how to party on a budget. From bingo nights to tai chi classes, I'm busier now than I was when I was working, and I'm not spending a dime. Well, except on the occasional cup of coffee."*

5. Healthcare: Plan for the Big Expenses

We've already covered some healthcare costs in earlier chapters, but when you're living on Social Security, planning for medical expenses becomes even more critical. Medicare helps, but it doesn't cover everything, and unexpected health issues can eat up your budget if you're not prepared.

How to Do It: Make sure you budget for Medicare premiums, out-of-pocket costs, and any supplemental insurance you might need. And don't forget about dental, vision, and hearing expenses; Medicare doesn't cover those, and they can sneak up on you faster than a surprise root canal.

Tip: *"I didn't think much about my teeth until I cracked a molar on a bagel. Turns out, dental work isn't cheap when you're on Medicare. Now I've got a budget line for 'surprise medical bills,' because you never know when your chompers are going to betray you."*

6. Keep a Small Emergency Fund

Even on Social Security, it's important to have a little cushion for those unexpected moments; car repairs, home maintenance, or that random time your water heater decides it's had enough. An emergency fund gives you peace of mind, even when you're on a fixed income.

How to Do It: Start small; aim for $500, then work your way up to $1,000. You don't have to save it all at once, but having a little set aside will help you avoid dipping into your monthly Social Security check when something comes up.

Tip: *"I always thought I didn't need an emergency fund because, well, what emergencies could possibly happen in retirement? Then my furnace broke in the middle of January, and let me tell you, that's one emergency I wasn't prepared for. Now I keep a little stash just for moments like that."*

7. Stay Social Without Spending a Fortune

One of the best parts of retirement is having the time to hang out with friends and family. But let's be honest, socializing can get expensive dinners out, movies, weekend trips. Luckily, there are plenty of ways to stay connected without burning through your Social Security check.

How to Do It: Host potlucks instead of going out to eat, organize game nights at home, or plan free outings like hikes or picnics. Most communities have free or low-cost events, and local senior centers often host get-togethers for little to no cost.

Tip: *"I used to blow my budget taking friends out for lunch. Then I got smart and started hosting card games at my house. Now, we play poker with pennies, and whoever loses must make the sandwiches. Cheap, fun, and no one has to worry about a bill at the end."*

CLOSING THOUGHTS: STRETCH IT LIKE YOU MEAN IT

Living on Social Security may feel like a balancing act, but with the right approach, you can make those dollars stretch further than you ever thought possible. By budgeting smart, cutting costs, and making the most of your benefits, you can live comfortably and even have a little fun along the way. Remember, retirement isn't about how much money you have; it's about making the most of what you've got. And trust me, you've got this.

CHECKLIST FOR LIVING ON SOCIAL SECURITY:

- Create a budget that covers your essentials and leaves room for some fun.

- Check for additional benefits like spousal or survivor Social Security.

- Cut costs where you can; senior discounts, downsizing, and thrifting.

- Embrace simple, low-cost hobbies to stay active and engaged.

- Budget for healthcare expenses and consider supplemental insurance.

- Keep a small emergency fund for unexpected expenses.

Chapter 10

Crisis Budgeting
MANAGING THE UNEXPECTED

EMERGENCY FUND MANAGEMENT

- **What is an Emergency Fund?**: A dedicated savings account set aside for unexpected expenses. Aim to save at least three to six months' worth of living expenses.

- **How to Build an Emergency Fund**: Start small by setting aside a portion of your income each month. Use automatic transfers to make saving easier.

- **When to Use Your Emergency Fund**: Know the difference between a true emergency (like medical bills or car repairs) and non-essential expenses. Establish criteria for using these funds to prevent premature depletion.

ADJUSTING BUDGETS

Assess Your Current Budget: Identify which expenses are fixed and which are variable. Focus on cutting non-essential spending to free up cash.

Create a Crisis Budget: Draft a bare-bones budget that prioritizes essentials; housing, food, utilities, and necessary medical care. This temporary budget should allow you to navigate through tough times without unnecessary stress.

ACTION PLAN
CUT NON-ESSENTIAL SPENDING

- Make a list of all your monthly expenses and categorize them into "needs" and "wants."

- Temporarily eliminate or reduce spending in the "wants" category. Consider postponing subscriptions, dining out, or entertainment expenses.

- Seek alternatives for enjoyment that are low-cost or free, such as community events or at-home activities.

Handle Emergencies

Immediate Steps to Take: If you face an unexpected expense, review your emergency fund first. If it's not sufficient, consider reaching out to family or friends for short-term support.

Stay Informed: Keep abreast of local and national resources that can assist during emergencies. This includes food banks, local charities, and online community support groups.

Using Government Resources

Research available government assistance programs that provide temporary relief for those in crisis, such as unemployment benefits, food assistance (SNAP), and utility assistance programs.

Learn how to apply for these resources efficiently to minimize delays in receiving help.

STRATEGIES FOR LONG-TERM FINANCIAL RESILIENCE

Strengthen Your Financial Foundation

Continuously contribute to your emergency fund, even during stable financial periods. This ensures you're always prepared for the unexpected.

Diversify income sources by exploring side gigs, freelance opportunities, or passive income streams.

Invest in Yourself

Consider taking courses or workshops to develop new skills that can enhance your employability. This investment can pay off in greater job security and higher income potential.

Regularly Review Your Financial Plan

Set a schedule to review your budget and financial goals regularly. This practice helps you stay on track and adjust to any changes in your financial situation.

Establish a financial support network: Surround yourself with financially savvy individuals or join local financial literacy groups to share experiences and advice.

RESOURCES AND BUDGETING TOOLS

As you start your budgeting journey, here are some useful tools and resources to help you stay on track. From budgeting apps to financial calculators and government programs, these tools will make managing your money easier and more effective.

Budgeting Apps:

- **Mint**
  A free app that helps you track spending, set budgets, and manage your bills. Mint links to your bank accounts and automatically categorizes your expenses, so you always know where your money is going.
  Website: mint.intuit.com

- **You Need a Budget (YNAB)**
  YNAB is a paid budgeting app that teaches you how to give every dollar a job and plan for future expenses. It's great for people who want a more hands-on approach to budgeting.
  Website: ynab.com

- **PocketGuard**
  A simple budgeting app that shows how much money you have left after accounting for bills, goals, and necessities. It's perfect for those who want an easy, visual way to manage their cash flow.
  Website: pocketguard.com

- **EveryDollar**
  Created by Dave Ramsey, EveryDollar is a budgeting app designed to help you create a monthly budget in just a few minutes. You can track your spending and make sure you're sticking to your plan.
  Website: everydollar.com

FINANCIAL CALCULATORS:

Retirement Savings Calculator
This calculator helps you estimate how much you'll need to save for retirement based on your current savings, retirement age, and expected expenses.
Website: nerdwallet.com/retirement-calculator

Social Security Benefits Calculator
Get an estimate of your future Social Security benefits based on your earnings history and when you plan to retire.
Website: ssa.gov/benefits/retirement/estimator

401(k) Withdrawal Calculator
Use this tool to determine how much you can withdraw from your 401(k) without depleting your savings too quickly.
Website: bankrate.com/retirement/401k-calculator

College Savings Calculator
If you're planning for your kids' education, this tool will help you estimate how much you need to save to cover future college costs.
Website: finaid.org/calculators

GOVERNMENT RESOURCES
RETIREMENT AND SOCIAL SECURITY:

Social Security Administration (SSA)
The official government site where you can apply for Social Security benefits, check your earnings record, and get estimates of your future benefits.
Website: ssa.gov

🧑 Medicare

Medicare provides healthcare coverage for people over 65. Learn about the different parts of Medicare, how to sign up, and what's covered.
Website: medicare.gov

🧑 Eldercare Locator

A government resource that helps seniors find services in their communities, such as housing, healthcare, and financial assistance programs.
Website: eldercare.acl.gov

🧑 BenefitsCheckUp

A service provided by the National Council on Aging that helps seniors find government programs they qualify for, such as food assistance, housing support, and healthcare benefits.
Website: benefitscheckup.org

These tools and resources will help you manage your budget, plan for retirement, and ensure you're taking full advantage of available programs. Remember, the more you know about your finances, the better equipped you'll be to handle any challenges that come your way. Happy budgeting!

Conclusion

FINAL WORDS ON BUDGETING

As we wrap up this journey through "**Budget Like a Boss**," it's important to reflect on what you've learned and how you can apply it to your financial life. Budgeting isn't just about numbers; it's about gaining control and flexibility over your money, which ultimately empowers you to live the life you want.

KEY TAKEAWAYS:

Financial Control: A solid budget gives you the power to allocate your resources effectively, ensuring that you can cover your needs, save for your future, and enjoy your life today.

Flexibility: Life is unpredictable, and a well-structured budget allows you to adapt to changes—whether that's navigating a financial crisis or seizing new opportunities.

THE EMOTIONAL SIDE OF MONEY

Money is not just a tool; it carries emotions and meanings unique to each of us. Understanding the emotional side of money can help you manage your finances more effectively. Here are a few insights:

- **Recognize Emotional Spending**: Be aware of how your feelings can influence your purchasing decisions. Stress, happiness, or boredom can lead to impulse buys that derail your budget.

- **Set Financial Goals**: Having clear, meaningful financial goals can motivate you to stick to your budget and resist the urge to overspend. Whether it's saving for a home, a dream vacation, or a comfortable retirement, keeping your goals in mind can help steer your financial decisions.

- **Practice Mindfulness**: Before making a purchase, take a moment to ask yourself: "Is this a need or a want? How will this impact my budget?" Mindfulness in spending can foster healthier financial habits.

YOUR NEXT STEPS
TAKE CONTROL OF YOUR FINANCIAL FUTURE

Now that you have the tools and knowledge to budget effectively, it's time to take action. Here's how to move forward:

- **Set Up Your Budget**: Create your personalized budget using the principles and techniques outlined in this book. Start with the 50/30/20 rule or your preferred method and adjust it to fit your lifestyle.

- **Automate Your Savings**: Make saving easier by automating transfers to your savings accounts. This simple step helps you prioritize your financial goals without having to think about it.

- **Build Your Emergency Fund**: Focus on building an emergency fund that covers 3-6 months of living expenses. This fund will provide a safety net during unexpected financial challenges.

- **Regularly Review and Adjust**: Make it a habit to review your budget regularly. Life changes, and so will your financial situation. Be prepared to adjust your budget to reflect these changes and stay on track.

- **Seek Support and Resources**: Don't hesitate to reach out for help or use financial resources available to you. Join financial literacy workshops, consult with a financial advisor, or engage with online communities focused on personal finance.

EXPLORE SELF HELP TITLES

Take a journey through collection of self-help books, where life's challenges are met with wisdom, humor, and practical advice.

Each title is designed to empower and guide readers through various aspects of personal and professional growth:

◊ [Bouncing Back: Resilience for Life's Curveballs](#)
Discover practical strategies for building resilience and facing life's unexpected challenges head-on, helping you grow stronger from adversity.

◊ [Adulting Guide: Failing, Learning, and Thriving](#)
Navigate the complexities of adulthood with real-life lessons, humorous anecdotes, and practical advice to help you thrive through challenges and failures.

◊ **The Entrepreneur's Playbook:** Strategies for Success
Equip yourself with actionable insights and strategies for entrepreneurship, covering everything from market
research to leadership and creating a lasting legacy.

With decades of experience across various fields, self-help books combine relatable stories, hard-earned wisdom, and practical steps to empower your personal and professional journey.

<u>Author Bio</u>

Aaron B. Kershaw is an author, mentor, and former U.S. Marine whose mission is to empower others through resilience, financial education, and practical life skills. With a diverse career spanning corporate leadership, media production, and community service, Aaron combines humor, insight, and hard-earned wisdom in his writing. 

His early experience managing a business as a high school student laid the groundwork for a lifelong dedication to helping others, a path that led him to significant roles with organizations like Habitat for Humanity and Guiding Eyes for the Blind.

A formerly-licensed financial advisor, insurance professional, and educator, Aaron has guided individuals and businesses through complex financial landscapes, helping them make informed decisions and reach their goals.

Known for his straightforward and relatable approach, he focuses on making life's toughest concepts more accessible and actionable. Beyond business and self-help, Aaron also writes teen thrillers, captivating younger audiences with suspenseful, action-packed stories.

Through his books, Aaron inspires readers of all ages to navigate life's unexpected twists, grow from every setback, and build a life of resilience and purpose.